The Indian Army

By Myauk

This edition Copyright Gosling Press 2025
All rights reserved.
ISBN 978-1-874351-36-8

Gosling Press
www.goslingpress.co.uk

The Indian Army A.B.C.

Being a record of some of those depressing events that occur in the daily life of every Officer of the INDIAN ARMY.

Introduction

This charming publication was originally published in 1915. The book claims to be from actual experience and although some of the text feels a little difficult to modern sensibilities, it is book is of its time and shines a light-hearted look at the Indian Army of the first World war

Myauk was a pseudonym for Captain John William Jerome Alves, originally Commissioned into the King's Own Scottish Borderers as a 2nd Lieutenant on 11 Aug 1900. He was later promoted to Lieutenant on 11 Nov 1902.

He transferred to the Indian Army on 13 Feb 1907 and was posted to the 93rd Burma Infantry. Promoted to Captain on 11 Aug 1909 and again to Major on 1 Sep 1915. He was a Double Company Officer in the Regiment in 1914.

The 93rd Burma Infantry was stationed at Barrackpore, Calcutta when WW1 started and were sent first to Egypt to protect the Suez Canal, then to France to join the Indian Expeditionary Force A and at the end of 1915 were redeployed to Mesopotamia. They arrived in time to take part in the failed efforts to relieve the besieged British garrison at Kut, and were present at the Battle of Sheikh Sa'ad (6-8 Jan 1916), the Battle of the Wadi (13 Jan 1916), the Battle of Hanna (21 Jan 1915) and the Battle of Dujaila Redoubt (8 Mar 1916) with the Regiment suffering over 400 casualties. In Dec 1916 they were part of the renewed advance up the Tigris River to Baghdad and were at the capture of Baghdad in Mar 1917. The Regiment was redeployed to Palestine and took part in the Battle Megiddo 19-25 Sep 1918. Major Alves died in Delhi on 29 Oct 1918 and was buried in the Delhi War Cemetery, New Delhi.

PREFACE.

DEAR READERS,

A few words as to the *raison d'etre* of this booklet may not be out of place.

Many a time and oft since joining the Indian Army have I been struck by the abysmal ignorance of "hoi polloi" as to the daily life of an officer in that glorious department. It seemed to me that too much could not be known of the subject by the general public, and after long consideration I decided to take it upon myself to turn on the necessary searchlight. The interest of the aforementioned "hoi polloi," said I to myself, will be best aroused by a series of stirring Indian military pictures depicting scenes taken from actual experience, and accompanied by arresting and apt quotations from the works of our foremost poets. But here arose a difficulty. The late Poet Laureate, having joined the majority, was not available; and though the couplets in this book will be universally ascribed to him, I hasten to inform you that they are scintillating gems which I was, in my extremity, forced to extract from the vast jewel-case of my own brain.

Now, if I may be allowed to say a few words as to my individual fitness for the task of producing this book, I would beg to point out that I am qualified by a military heredity. My great-uncle, the great General Sir W. Ashout (who suffered during the latter years of his service from convergent strabismus and pronounced and chronic hepatic nodules), revolutionised the musketry of his day by the substitution of Palaeolithic for Devonian flints in the sparking plugs of the arquebus (Mark IV. * ᵈ/10.3.1702, 500,000, W. & S.), whilst my grandfather will long b remembered as the inventor of the modern Emergency Ration, which consists of two adamantin cakes of discoloured granite, the one labelled "Soup," and the other "Chocolate." Both ar entirely insoluble in water, and are so devised as to be usable either as ammunition for a fougass, o in larger quantities, as metal for what are known as "10 minute roads" (the type of thoroughfa now universally adopted by the Public Works Department).

Lastly, my uncle on my mother's side, a famous General of Bengal Engineers, originate the method, now exclusively employed by the sepoy, of making fine adjustments in the machinery of a maxim gun or heliograph by means of the head of a pickaxe. However, great as was his influence with the *personnel* of the Native Army, he failed, during a career of over 40 years, to attain the ambition of his life, which was to educate the sepoy to such a pitch of erudition as to enable him to take up any photograph and at once regard it right side up.

Suffering, as he did, from the ravages of an insidious disease induced by a taste for a little known Eastern drug, yclept by apothecaries $C_2 H_5 O H$, the immediate cause of his sudden dematerialisation was one Ganda Singh, a sepoy, who, when shown by my uncle a photograph of the latest "Dreadnought," held it upside down, and thoughtfully remarked, "Bahut achcha bāngla."

A's the Adjēētant—his principal duty's to make fighting men out of jungly rungruties.

H stands for Hockey
a pastime that serves

as a capital method of testing the nerves.

K IS FOR "KUSHTI"—
 WE HERE SEE TWO SEPOYS—
EACH TRYING TO UPSET
 THE OTHER'S EQUIPOISE.

L IS A FOLLOWER KNOWN AS A "LANGRI"—

HE APPEARS ON THE SCENE

WHEN THE SEPOYS ARE HUNGRY

M for M.I. that most mobile of forces

Which works, now and then,

quite apart from its horses.

Q is the Quoit, which is used by the Sikhs
for sending their enemies
over the Styx.

X is an asinine sort of a Letter; No words begin with it. (So much the better!)

Y for the Youth who with pitying sniggers, Looks on our Sepoys as so many "Niggers".